Dogs
at Work

Julia Barnes

GARETH**STEVENS,**INC.

GS

A Member of the WRC Media Family of Companies

Please visit our Web site at: www.garethstevens.com
For a free color catalog describing Gareth Stevens Publishing's list of high-quality books and multimedia programs, call 1-800-542-2595 (USA) or 1-800-387-3178 (Canada). Gareth Stevens Publishing's fax: (414) 332-3567.

Library of Congress Cataloging-in-Publication Data

Barnes, Julia, 1955-
    Dogs at work / Julia Barnes.— North American ed.
      p. cm. — (Animals at work)
    Includes bibliographical references and index.
    ISBN 0-8368-6223-6 (lib. bdg.)
    1. Working dogs—Juvenile literature. I. Title.
  SF428.2.B37 2006
  636.7'0886—dc22   2005054068

This North American edition first published in 2006 by
Gareth Stevens Publishing
A Member of the WRC Media Family of Companies
330 West Olive Street, Suite 100
Milwaukee, WI 53212 USA

This U.S. edition copyright © 2006 by Gareth Stevens, Inc. Original edition copyright © 2005 by Westline Publishing, The Warren, Aylburton, Lydney, Gloucestershire, GL15 6DX.

Gareth Stevens editor: Carol Ryback
Gareth Stevens designer: Charlie Dahl

Photo Credits:
Guide Dogs for the Blind Association: 1, 4, 28, 29. Ruthann McCaulley: 5 (top). Michael R. Meyering 5 (bottom). Annelies Roeterdink: 9. Defence Animal Centre: 11, 18. Metropolitan Police 12. Bob Eden, PoliceK9/Eden Consulting Group: 13, 14, 15. HM Revenue and Customs: 16. PDSA: 19. AQIS, Australian Government: 20, 21. Search Dog Foundation: 22, 23, 24. Allen Parton — Canine Partners: 25, 26, 27, 28. Dogs for the Disabled: 25, 26. Hearing Dogs for Deaf People: 27.

Special thanks to Captain Gus Moulas and K-9 Officer Qai of the Elm Grove Police Department in Elm Grove, Wisconsin.

Printed in the United States of America

1 2 3 4 5 6 7 8 9 10 09 08 07 06

Contents

Introduction

After training together, the guide dog and its owner form a close partnership.

A blind man is ready to step off a train. He asks his guide dog to go forward, but the dog refuses to move, despite repeated commands. Just then, a railroad official comes rushing up.

"Your dog saved you from falling onto the track," the official says.

The amazing partnership between a person with disabilities and his or her guide dog is only one example of the way dogs and humans work as teams.

We train dogs to use their sense of smell, their intelligence, and, perhaps most importantly, their devotion, to help us perform a wide variety of complex tasks.

Find out about:

- Police dogs that go after armed criminals.
- Search dogs that work tirelessly to find survivors of disasters.
- Detector dogs that indicate drugs and explosives.
- Guide dogs that provide independence for their blind owners (*pictured left*).
- Hearing dogs that alert their owners to household sounds.

Dogs At Work examines the range of tasks that dogs perform, reviews the required training methods, and explains which **canines** are best suited to the particular jobs mentioned.

Coming In from the Wild

The first dogs to work for us

Compare an Irish wolfhound and a Chihuahua — and you can hardly believe that they are the same **species**. Although hundreds of different dog breeds exist — the American Kennel Club recognizes more than 150 breeds — all canines descended from the same wild animal: the wolf.

The wolf originated about two million years ago. This small, meat-eating hunter was so successful that its range spread throughout North America, Asia, and Europe. The wolf's links with people began ten thousand years ago when the first wolves began hanging around humans. In return for food and shelter, the wolves helped with the hunt and guarded the home. Newborn wolf pups became playmates for children, and so — as time passed — the wolf became **domesticated**, sharing life with its human family.

Dogs today

Domesticated dogs are even more useful to us today than ever before. Certain breeds work at specialized tasks better than others. We constantly find more ways that dogs can assist us in our daily lives. Even when a dog is not working, it makes a difference by giving the companionship and love that makes it a human's best friend.

All dogs, including the Irish wolfhound (above) and the tiny, long-haired Chihuahua (below) are descended from the wolf.

The Herders

The unchanging role of working sheepdogs

When dogs first came to live with humans thousands of years ago, they were used to help with the hunt, to herd and protect **livestock**, and to guard the home.

Over time, our needs have changed. We have selected certain breeds to train for a variety of tasks. After proper training, these animals become specialists in their fields.

On the farm

Border collies are the best herders of sheep. No machines equal them. Quick-thinking, skillful and obedient, the border collie is a tireless worker that spends long, hard days alongside its master.

Originally bred in the border counties of England and Scotland, the border collie is now the number one herding dog in North America, Australia, and New Zealand.

Working on instinct

Border collies, and some of the other working breeds, such as Australian shepherds, are born with the **instinct** to herd.

If you watch a puppy from one of these breeds, it will crouch down and fix its eyes on whatever object it

A border collie is trained to work in partnership with the shepherd.

A border collie creeps up on the sheep as it gets ready to herd them.

thinks it should "herd." The dog might choose an animal to herd, but it might also choose to herd its toys!

A cattle farmer helps a dog develop and fine-tune its instinct to herd sheep. Using voice commands or whistles, the farmer will teach his dog to:
• move left or right.

• quietly creep up behind the sheep and gather them together.
• drive the sheep in the direction the farmer wants them to go.
• separate some of the sheep from the herd.
• guide the sheep to a safe enclosure.

A well-trained dog makes such tasks look easy, but both the farmer and the dog work hard to achieve those goals. Careful, repetitive training produces a first-rate sheep-herding dog.

Some farmers eagerly show off their dogs' skills by entering them in sheep-herding trials, which are often highly competitive, international events.

DID YOU KNOW

Farmers in Australia wanted a tough, determined breed of dog that could drive cattle across their huge, open ranches. The Australian cattle dog was bred to herd livestock. The dogs run behind the cattle, nipping at their heels if they try to slow down.

The Australian cattle dog is bred to herd cattle.

Sporting Companions

Teamwork on the hunting field

The days when most humans had to depend on hunting for their food are long gone. Many "sport" hunters, however, use dogs when they track, shoot, and kill game birds for extra food or as a leisure activity.

Sport hunters work with their animals to train them to assist with the hunt.

Born to retrieve

Dogs instinctively use the same skills their ancestors used when hunting for food.
- A hunting dog follows the scent of an animal on the ground or picks up a scent carried in the air.
- The dog "freezes" when it finds an animal, so it does not alert its **prey**.
- After a kill, the dog brings the prey to its handler.

When dogs first came to live with humans, they helped with all aspects of the hunt. With the invention of

Labrador retrievers gently carry the shot game as they retrieve it.

DID YOU KNOW
Retrievers, and a number of the spaniel breeds, are excellent swimmers. They will plunge into freezing cold water to retrieve a shot bird.

The Irish water spaniel is as much at home in water as on land.

the shotgun, the dog's role changed to finding the prey animal and **retrieving** it. The best working dogs were bred with each other.
In time, dog breeds with specialized hunting skills were created. Sporting breeds used by today's hunters are highly valued. These dogs include the following breeds:

- *Spaniels* (English springer spaniel, cocker spaniel, Irish water spaniel): energetic dogs that disappear into the undergrowth, noses to the ground, to flush out or retrieve game.

- *Pointers and setters* (pointer, Irish setter, English setter): athletic dogs that pick up scents in the air and freeze when they find game.

- *Retrievers* (Labrador retriever, golden retriever, flat-coated retriever): hard-working dogs that stay close to their handler and wait until ordered to retrieve it.

European hunters wanted a general-purpose dog that could perform all the duties of a shooting companion.

They developed a number of breeds that could hunt, point, and retrieve. These working dogs, which include Weimaraners and German shorthaired pointers, are now also popular choices for hunting dogs in North America as well.

The German shorthaired pointer freezes to show it found a bird.

The Front Line

Heroic dogs that serve in the military

Dogs are called on to help their human owners in all situations, even in wartime. The mighty mastiff was the first dog of war. Ancient Romans dressed dogs in armor, and these fierce dogs fought alongside their masters. The first military dog training school was set up in Germany in the late nineteenth century. After that, dogs played an increasingly active role in wartime.

Under fire

During World War I (1914–1918), a number of different breeds were chosen to serve the military, including German shepherds, boxers, and airedale terriers. These active and intelligent dogs served many roles:

- Guard dogs: Army dogs would **patrol** with their handlers and **alert** them to any hidden enemy. Dogs also guarded prisoners of war.
- Messenger dogs: Dogs were trained to take messages to different sections of the army, which often helped save lives. The dogs could run much faster than soldiers, especially over muddy ground.
- Search dogs: Dogs were used to find injured soldiers in thick woodland.

Roll of honor

Dogs not only carried out their duties, but also showed great bravery. This was particularly true during World War II (1939–1945). Dogs that showed outstanding courage were awarded special medals.

Some of the decorated dogs included:

- Kurt, a Doberman, saved the lives of 250 Marines in the Battle of Guam when he alerted them to Japanese soldiers hiding ahead.

Airedale terriers were used as messengers during WWI.

Dogs continue to play an important military role in modern armed forces around the world.

- Chips, a German shepherd **mixed breed**, who served with the U.S. Army in Sicily, attacked an enemy machine-gun crew, forcing them to surrender.
- Brian, a German shepherd and a member of Britain's elite Special Air Service, made more than twenty parachute drops (equipped with a special harness and parachute) to work on secret missions behind enemy lines in France.

A modern role

Today, dogs are used by armies all over the world for guard and patrol work and increasingly to search for land mines and explosives (*see pages 18-19*). Dogs and their military handlers must be ready for active duty at all times. This often involves trips overseas to countries where dogs are serving with forces from the United States, Britain, and other countries.

see pages 18-19

DID YOU KNOW
Canine war memorials honor the bravery of dogs who served in wartime. The United States has canine memorials on both coasts, as well as on the Pacific island of Guam. They honor the dogs that lost their lives when serving with the U.S. armed forces.

Army dog and handler teams are prepared to travel all over the world.

On Patrol

K-9 "officers" join the fight against crime

A police dog must spring into action the moment its handler gives the command. Patrol dogs can stop or corner even the most determined criminal.

Police departments around the world use dogs in many different ways: on patrol to keep order, searching property or looking for people (*see page 15*),

Someday, this German shepherd puppy may train as a police dog.

and catching escaped criminals. Police dogs also perform the highly specialized work of finding explosives and drugs (*see pages 14–19*).

Dogs become canine officers in a number of ways. Some police departments contract with certified breeders, who breed certain dogs for desired traits. Puppies that will become police dogs spend their first year in private homes learning basic obedience tasks, just like dogs that are pets. Other potential police dogs may be rescued from shelters. Once formal police training starts, the future police dogs live with their handlers. As the dog and handler go through advanced training together, a strong **bond** develops between them.

A police dog undergoes strict training that includes learning when to attack.

A police dog undergoes strict training that includes learning when to attack.

Police dog training

What we consider training is "playing" to a dog. As the dog learns tasks, it thinks it is playing a game. A dog cannot understand the idea of crime. When a police dog chases someone or looks for something, it does so because that is what the handler ordered — and, by following its handler's commands, the dog gets a **reward**.

The handler rewards a dog for a successfully completed task with a game, such as tug-of-war or fetch, using its favorite toy. Dogs do not receive edible rewards. Criminals often try to conceal, or disguise, the smell of illegal drugs or explosives with normal food items, such as a hamburger, candy, or coffee grounds.

Types of training

A police dog undergoes a variety of training techniques. **Agility** training not only teaches the dog to jump over hurdles and other obstacles, but also improves the dog's overall fitness and strength. Dogs also learn different tracking methods, as well as how to hold a suspect without **mauling** him or her. The dog trains by attacking a "**decoy**"

or "**K-9 agitator**" — a highly trained instructor wearing padded equipment. The dog releases its hold on command of its handler.

> **DID YOU KNOW**
> A police dog does not always clearly understand when it is working and when it is "off duty." The handler is responsible for the animal's behavior at home and when out in public.

The Nose Knows

The amazing world of detector dogs

We humans cannot even begin to imagine all that a dog can smell. Recent studies found that most breeds of dogs have about 1 billion **scent cells** that detect odor (bloodhounds have about 4 billion), while humans have only about 12 million odor-detection cells. Dogs are trained to follow a **scent trail** over different surfaces. (The weather, temperature, and amount of vehicle traffic are only a few of the factors that can affect how long the scent trail lasts.) Dogs can also detect the smell of a body buried under an avalanche or trapped under piles of dirt and rubble.

Dogs are trained to follow the trail of a human's scent.

Dogs train under many conditions, including under heavy smoke cover.

We use the canines' incredible sense of smell many different ways.

Tracking dogs

Police and military dogs help find people and locate property.

A trained **tracking** dog follows a human scent trail. The dog's handler encourages it to follow the scent until it leads to the person or item being sought or until the scent disappears. Police or army patrol dogs may locate hiding criminals or enemy soldiers. The dog may also find an item of clothing worn by that person or some other possession — which often leads to the suspect's location.

The dog's sense of smell is so good that it can often follow older scent trails for long distances, especially in natural areas, such as a field or forest. Scent trails usually do not stay "fresh" for long on paved surfaces. Dog trackings are most sussessful when they begin following a trail that is only about thirty minutes old.

The dogs may follow a scent three main ways:
- sure tracking — nose to ground to follow footsteps.
- trailing — nose held slightly above ground to smell vapors.
- air scenting — nose up; the person is most likely very near.

Drug Detectors

Specialist dogs with a nose for drugs

Fighting drug crime is a major part of police work all over the world, and trained dogs play an important role in drug searches.

Customs agents in airports and seaports always watch for drug smuggling activities.

The customs agents search passengers, luggage, cars, boats, and cargo. Likewise, police often need to search suspects who may be carrying drugs. Sometimes, officers need to enter and search buildings where they think smugglers

hid the drugs. Drug detector dogs help the customs agents and police conduct these searches faster.

On the trail
Every drug has a definite scent. Police and customs dogs are trained to recognize

A detector dog picks up the scent of hidden drugs.

Detector dogs are trained to search unusual places. They also learn how to alert their handlers to the presence of drugs.

certain scents and then alert their handlers. The dogs are not harmed by sniffing the drugs. They smell chemicals given off by the drugs, but do not fall under the effects of the drugs.

The handler shows the dog where to begin a search and encourages it to keep going. A dog may do a repeat search of an area, if necessary. Search dogs indicate a find two ways:

• **passive indication** — The dog sits, lies down, or looks at whatever it finds.
• **active indication** — the dog points with its nose, barks, or scratches at its find.

Breed choice

Although the police traditionally use German shepherds, hunting breeds, including Labrador and golden retrievers and springer spaniels, are often used as detector dogs. Retrievers and spaniels instinctively follow scents. The springer, with a smaller and lighter build, works well in cramped conditions. Border collies also make great detector search dogs. Smugglers keep thinking of new places to hide drugs and outsmart the dogs' noses, but detector dogs manage to find the drugs anyway. Dogs have found drugs hidden in many odd places, including inside **piñatas**, surfboards, timber, religious headgear, melons, potatoes, light fixtures, and even fake limbs!

Bomb Alert!

Calling in the explosives search dogs

In World War II, dogs helped locate buried **land mines**, which saved many lives. Today, explosives search dogs play an important role to help guard against the worldwide threat of **terrorist attacks**.

Security special

Police forces, the different branches of the military, and customs agents often need to locate weapons and explosives that are stashed or carried for criminal or terrorist activities. Explosives search dogs serve as invaluable assistants.

All explosives and firearms give off distinct odors. A dog learns to recognize those scents and alert its handler. The dog also learns to recognize the scent of ammunition and bomb-making equipment. Training is intensive — a dog may conduct a long search but find nothing. The handler must encourage the dog to continue.

Dogs selected for this training must be energetic, responsive to their handler, and love to play. Their reward for alerting a handler to a stash of weapons is often a favorite toy. The dog signals a find by sitting or lying still. Handlers train their dogs to stay well away from their find, for many types of weapons and explosives could prove highly dangerous to the dog. Handlers want to keep their dogs as safe as possible.

An explosives-detecting dog can save many lives.

Buster, shown with handler Sergeant Danny Morgan, received a medal for his remarkable work.

Buster, the hero

Buster, a five-year-old English springer spaniel, served in the British army. He was sent to work in Iraq with his handler, Sergeant Danny Morgan. Like all the troops, Buster and Danny faced the constant danger of attack from terrorists. One day, Buster and Danny participated in a surprise dawn raid in enemy territory.

As Danny says: "The soldiers had found nothing, so I unleashed Buster to see if he could detect anything. Within minutes, he became very excited and I knew we had discovered something."

The soldiers knocked down a wall to reveal a huge weapons **cache**, including grenades and bomb-making equipment.

The stash of weapons belonged to a terrorist group. It was large enough to kill perhaps thousands of people. Following Buster's discovery, attacks on the British troops stopped in that area.

Back in Britain, Buster received a medal for his outstanding devotion to duty. "He's my best friend — and my hero," says Danny.

Other members of military canine units feel the same way about their animals. Buster is only one of many valuable canines serving with armed forces throughout the world.

Beagle Brigade

Protecting nations against the dangers of disease

As we have seen, "detector dogs" (*pages 14–19*) help find illegal substances, such as explosives or drugs, that might be smuggled into a country. Other items, such as meat, plants, and vegetables — that at first seem perfectly harmless — may carry insect or other animal pests, as well as diseases, that can spread to new countries with disastrous results.

Customs agents in the United States, Canada, Australia, and other countries, take great care to ensure that risky items are not brought in with passengers' luggage. Customs agents get a lot of help from the Beagle Brigade.

Natural dangers?
Beagles' fantastic sense of smell makes them the perfect breed for work as detector dogs for **quarantined** items. The beagles learn to identify up to thirty different quarantined items, which may include any of the following natural products that could harm native products:

DID YOU KNOW
Beagle Brigade teams work in at least twenty-one U.S. border crossing areas, ports, and international airports. Customs agents seize about 75,000 banned food items annually.

The beagle must search every item of luggage that is presented to it.

A detector dog must ignore all smells except those that it has been trained to find.

This Beagle sits to indicate that it found a target odor.

- fresh fruit and vegetables
- meat — fresh, canned, and processed
- plants and plant cuttings
- eggs
- soil
- seeds
- dairy products

Learning the skills

Much the same way that drug detecting dogs and explosive detecting dogs learn to indicate a find, instructors of the Beagle Bridgade usually teach each dog to sit as soon as it finds a scent. For an active response, the beagle might react by barking or pawing at a box containing a banned item or foodstuff.

As training progresses, the beagle practices finding a **target odor** among suitcases and other items of luggage. With experience, the beagle learns to respond to a wide range of illegal items that people smuggle. After the training course is completed, members of the Beagle Brigade go to work at border crossings.

Beagles excel at identifying agricultural (farm) products, so they are the breed of choice for such duties.

Dogs that find forbidden fruit, meat, or vegetables are rewarded by playing a game of tug-of-war.

> ### DID YOU KNOW
> The U.S. government uses middle-sized breeds, such as Labrador or golden retrievers, to work in post offices and seaports. These dogs also back up the Beagle Brigade at international airports.

Searching for Survivors

Dogs called in after a natural disaster

Saint Bernards were the first canines used as search and rescue dogs. In the 1700s, Swiss monks started working with dogs to find travelers lost in the Alps. The Saint Bernard dogs, which could sniff out people buried in avalanches, soon became famous.

Over the next three hundred years, Saint Bernards saved more than two thousand lives.

Helicopter search-and-rescue teams have since replaced the huge, friendly dogs. The use of dogs for search and rescue, meanwhile, has expanded and changed to involve far more than mountain peaks and deep snow.

When disaster strikes

Emergency service personnel are fully activated whenever a natural disaster — such as an earthquake, a flood, or an avalanche — occurs, and an immediate search for survivors begins. A train derailment or a terrorist attack causes a similar type of emergency search-and-rescue team response.

Search Dog Foundation canine-firefighter teams traveled to Ground Zero in New York City.

LA Times

DID YOU KNOW

A search dog picks up the scent of a buried person because a human body gives off an odor that rises to the surface.

A human handler encourages disaster search dog *Recon* to climb over boulders.

© Kristen Mahoney

Howard Orr and canine partner *Duke* practice *rapelling*.

Disaster search dogs play an important role during such events. These dogs are trained to find one scent — humans buried under objects. The dogs work tirelessly, often in difficult and dangerous conditions, alongside their human partners, who are generally firefighters or members of other emergency rescue services. When a dog finds the scent of a trapped human, it alerts the handler by barking. A second dog is often called in to confirm the find. Rescue workers must carefully remove whatever is covering the person in order to prevent further harm.

Courageous canines

It takes a very special dog to work in disaster areas. Strength, agility, and **endurance** are essential. A disaster situation often requires working long hours in hazardous conditions. The dog must not be timid or frighten easily. It may need to work in a partially collapsed building, climb over broken glass and jagged debris, or balance itself on narrow, uneven, or unstable surfaces.

Many different organizations and individuals all over the world train search dogs. The Search Dog

Dusty **practices agility and balance by walking across the "wobbly monster."**

Disaster search dog *Trapper* climbs a ladder during training.

Foundation, located in Ojai, California, is one of the largest of its kind in the United States. The Search Dog Foundation (SDF) chooses and trains shelter dogs that exhibit certain behaviors.

They look for dogs with these qualities:
- high energy
- friendliness
- playfulness
- willingness to please

Training is based on the dog's desire to find a toy. A good working dog will do anything for the reward of a game with a favorite toy.

Early training begins in a family "prep home," followed by six months of specialized, advanced obedience and disaster search skills training.

Each dog is then matched with a human partner. The SDF wants the dog and handler to form a strong bond. The handler must develop complete trust in the dog, and, likewise, the dog develop complete trust in its handler.

After a period of training, every new team is ready to start work and meet the many challenges of searching for survivors of natural or human-caused disasters.

Assistance Dogs

Dogs that help people with disabilities

Assistance dogs train for a variety of tasks to help people with disabilities meet everyday challenges. The dogs learn how to help their owners perform simple actions, such as opening doors, getting dressed, or answering the telephone.

After about one year of basic obedience training, assistance dogs enter advanced training to learn how to assist people with specific disabilities. The dogs are taught to assist someone who is confined to a wheelchair, someone who is deaf, or someone who may have unique

health problems, such as the likelihood of having a seizure or heart attack.

Assistance dogs also remain aware of any potential dangers in the owner's immediate environment and learn how to respond and seek help if the owner loses consciousness.

Helping hounds . . .

1. remove clothes from a washing machine.

2. work an automatic teller machine (ATM).

3. assist with shopping chores.

Tom (left) with assistance dog, *Viggo*, and Kayleigh with her assistance dog, *Vicky*.

Assistance dog *Endal* gave Allen Parton the will to live after he was wounded in the Gulf War. *Endal* is now Allen's constant companion and helper.

Assistance dogs learn the following skills:

- Alerting — They make an owner aware of a ringing telephone, a doorbell, or a crying baby.
- Pressing — They learn to use a paw to operate a light switch, an automatic door, or an elevator alarm button.
- Pulling — They might need to pull a rope attached to a door handle or a cord attached to a light switch. Assistance dogs also learn to pull clothes from a washing machine and help their owner undress. They might even help their owner pull the wheelchair along.
- Retrieving — They fetch or pick up items the owner may drop.
- "Speaking" on command — They bark to alert others when their owner is in trouble.

Dogs are also trained to walk alongside a wheelchair to assist its owner at all times.

Helping children

Some assistance dogs are trained to work with children with disabilities. In this remarkably successful training, the children gain a new sense of purpose because — with the help of their parents — they are also responsible for caring for their dog.

A hearing dog alerts its owner to a sound . . .

. . . and then shows its owner what is making the sound.

An assistance dog can help a child in the following ways:

- The dog picks up items dropped by the child.
- The child gets exercise and an enjoyable type of physical therapy when he or she helps groom or plays with the dog.
- The dog sleeps in the child's room at night in order to alert the parents to any problems.

Hearing dogs

Hearing dogs alert their owners to everyday noises, such as alarm clocks, telephones, babies, doorbells, and smoke detectors. The dogs must show their owners what is making the sound so the owner knows how to react. Dogs that assist people with hearing difficulties also learn what to do for their owners while out in public. The animals watch for traffic and recognize other dangers that a person who cannot hear might not notice.

Hearing dogs respond to hand signals and verbal commands. Many hearing dogs are selected from shelters. Trainers seek out dogs that are naturally friendly and eager to please. The dogs may be nearly any breed and size, from Labrador retrievers to smaller terriers, and often include mixed breeds.

Guide Dogs

Dogs that act as eyes for their blind owners

Have you ever watched a guide dog calmly guide its blind owner through crowded streets or wait for traffic to pass before safely crossing a road? Such guidance requires a remarkable degree of skill and training because the dog is 100 percent responsible for its owner's safety.

Early days

Dogs were first trained as guides for the blind in Germany. During World War I, dogs that had been used to search for injured soldiers were retrained to work with soldiers who had been blinded in battle. This retraining was so successful that soon guide dog training schools appeared all over the world.

In harness

The first guide dogs were German shepherds, but now a variety of breeds are used. The most popular choices are Labrador retrievers, golden retrievers and Labrador-golden mixed breeds. These dogs are not only intelligent and eager to learn, but also calm, steady, and reliable.

Most guide dog puppies are reared by volunteers in private homes. At about fourteen months, the dogs leave their adoptive family and begin specialized training. The dogs are first trained to guide on a long lead, or leash, and later are fitted with a special **harness**. The guide-dog instructor teaches the animal:

• to walk at a steady pace in the guiding position.

Golden retrievers make wonderful guide dogs for the blind.

A trainee guide dog learns to walk around obstacles while leaving room for its handler.

A guide dog will not step off a curb unless it is safe to do so.

- to halt at curbs.
- to cross a road only when clear of traffic.
- to change direction.
- to notice and avoid various obstacles, such as traffic cones, holes in pavement, or objects that stick out above the dog's

head and blocks its owner's path.

After the initial guide dog training, which takes many months, the animal trains with its blind owner. As they work together, a lifelong partnership and bonding

develops, and the two become a team.

DID YOU KNOW

Dogs do not normally notice objects above their heads. Guide dogs learn how to watch for and avoid low branches, road signs, or ropes.

ELKHART LAKE I M D

Glossary

active indication: a moving alert to a handler, such as barking or pawing.

agility: the ability to move easily.

alert: a dog signaling to its handler.

bond: an emotional attachment.

canines: having to do with dogs.

cache: a stash or supply.

customs agents: officials who examine goods and baggage as people cross the borders of a country.

decoy (or **K-9 agitator**): a trainer pretending to be an attacker.

domesticated: cared for by people; no longer living in the wild.

endurance: to keep going without getting tired.

harness: the strappy equipment worn by a guide dog.

instinct: natural behavior.

land mine: an explosive buried just under the surface of the ground.

livestock: animals, such as sheep and cattle, that are raised for food.

mauling: fiercely biting and attacking an animal or person.

mixed breed: a dog whose mother and father are different breeds.

passive indication: a quiet behavior, such as sitting, to alert the handler.

patrol: a regular tour of an area to guard it and keep order.

piñatas: traditional Mexican hollow paper creatures that are filled with candy and toys.

prey: an animal that is attacked.

quarantined: forbidden from moving about freely.

rapelling: dropping from a high area by using ropes to control the descent.

retrieving: running after and bringing back an item to the handler.

reward: the praise, toy, or playtime used to reinforce a behavior.

scent cells: cells within the nose that detect odors.

scent trail: the odor left by a person, an item of clothing, or another animal, that a trained dog can follow.

species: a distinct biological group.

target odor: a scent that a dog is taught to recognize.

terrorist attacks: acts of violence, such as bombings, used in hopes of influencing a change in attitude or method of operation.

tracking: a dog following a scent trail.

Find Out More . . .

More books to read

Anderson, Bendix. *Search Dogs. Dog Heroes* (series). Bearport (2005).

George, Charles, and Linda. *Bomb Detection Dogs.* Capstone (1998).

Garfield, James B. *Follow My Leader.* Puffin (1994).

Lawrenson, Diana. *Guide Dogs: From Puppies to Partners.*
    Allen & Unwin, Limited (2002).

Ruffin, Frances E. *Police Dogs. Dog Heroes* (series). Bearport (2005).

Web sites

www.cia.gov/cia/ciakids/index_2.shtml
Visit the CIA's Web site on working dogs.

www.fbi.gov/kids/dogs/doghome.htm
Discover how the FBI puts special canine agents to work.

www.nhm.org/exhibitions/dogs/atd/therapy.html
Learn about the many kinds of therapy dogs.

www.usatechguide.org/techguide.php?vmode=1&catid=282
Follow the links to a variety of service and assistance dog organizations.

http://community.webtv.net/Hahn-50thAP-K9/K9History4/
Read the adventures of some of the dogs that fought in WWII.

Index